Purpose In My Pain

Genina Johnson

Purpose In My Pain

Genina Johnson

Firebrand Publishing

Purpose In My Pain

Genina Johnson

Cover design by Firebrand Publishing

Published Worldwide by Firebrand Publishing, Atlanta, Georgia,

First Edition, November, 2018

ISBN: 978-1-941907-09-2

https://firebrandpublishing.com

www.geninaj.com

Genina Johnson

DEDICATION

To my children Alex, Excell and McKenzie and my God Children Michael, Makiyah, Brooklyn, and Drake.

Remember that you can do all things through Christ who strengthens you!

Never allow anyone to make you lose sight of your worth. You are more than enough. I speak blessings and prosperity over your lives. Generational curses are being destroyed off your lives, and your blood line. You will obtain all that God has for you. Now Go change the world!

To my grandmother, I thank God for your life! God knew exactly what He was doing when He called my mommy home!

I thank you for being my ride or die. The love you have shown to me, my sister, my children, is the true agape love, God has shown us! I'm blessed to have you as my grandmother! My children are blessed as well.

1

Genina Johnson

To my family and friends, thanks for all your love and support during my journey and my story!

Thank you for sticking by my side when others left or had to be removed from the table. Everyone can't go with you to your next level in life. Well I'm glad you guys are coming with me. So, enjoy the ride!!!

Love always,
Gege

CHAPTER ONE

In The Beginning

y early years of growing were not bad at all. My grandparents were very nurturing people. We were very fortunate, and seemed to have what we needed. I was never forced to do without. My family was very close, and family oriented. We often had family reunions and BBQ's at my grandmother's house. That was the house where everyone would come to get together, laugh, eat and enjoy good times, as a family.

I believe I experienced my first parts of rejection when I was very young. As a young child, I yearned to have that father and daughter bond, but due to my father's history with drugs, his arrest, and legal troubles, that close father daughter relationship was difficult to have. At such an early age, when I was seven, my father was in and out of the prison system, and my mother was battling Scleroderma, an autoimmune illness that negatively impacts all major organs. It begins to harden all your major organs including the skin. Due to my mother's illness, she was not able to take care of me and my twin sister, Savannah. We were sent to live with my paternal grandparents. I always thanked God we didn't have to go into the foster care system.

I have always been a daddy's girl. I even look like my daddy. I can remember at the age of seven, when the police came into my grandmother's house to take my father into custody. I was screaming and hollering at the officers, "Please don't take my daddy away!"

This was a terrible time that I still remember clearly, all these years later. As I think about it, I believe that due to my father's absence as a child, I've been longing for the love and acceptance from men. So, due to the absence of my father, and my mother's failing health, my mother decided that it would be best

7 4 3 7 6

if Savannah and I move in with our grandparents.

I remember at the age of nine, it was my grandmother who first saw the light of God shining upon me. At the time, she was a grandmother of five, and she would always say, "Genina, you are so special!"

I never understood what kind of 'special' she was talking about, but it was finally revealed to me at the age of nineteen. My grandma was a gentle soul. She had a big heart and sometimes people would take advantage of her, because of her kindness, and love for people. I also have traits like my grandmother, although my grandmother was more strict than I am.

As children we couldn't go off the block and we couldn't accept phone calls either. Our cousins lived down the street from us. Their names were Brittany, Teyanna, and Samantha. They were really the only kids we were allowed to hang out with. Their grandmother was strict as well.

When I was thirteen, my mother passed away. My mother's death was very hard on my sister and I because we didn't understand how ill she really was.

I remember asking my mom if she was going to die, and if she was she was, taking us with her.

She told us no.

We would watch her have to feed herself through a tube because her G.I system was failing and she couldn't hold any food down. Her kidneys started failing which caused her to need dialysis. She would have these painful episodes where we would have to call the ambulance, which caused her to be hospitalized.

She died a few months before our eighth grade graduation.

Her death took a big toll on us, because my middle school graduation was a very special moment that my mother couldn't be a part of. Throughout my life, every special moment in my life has made me cry. I have cried because my mother was not physically present, although I know that she was there spiritually.

Savannah and I were very sheltered. After graduating from grammar school, we choose to attend a high school that was far from where we lived. High school really provided many memorable experiences, and I enjoyed it.

We attended Chicago Vocational Career Academy, better known as CVS. CVS high school is the largest high school in the city of Chicago. I was a member of the cheerleading team, then I joined the dancing dolls team.

We would participate in the battle of the bands, where we would would battle other high school bands. I remember if someone wanted to fight, they would pull the fire alarm so every one would have to exit the school, then all the fights would break out.

My grades were satisfactory in high school. They could have been better. I remember Savannah and I would use the excuse that we were still mourning the death of our mother, when we didn't get good grades. After a while our grandparents weren't having it. LOL.

We graduated from high school on schedule. We planned to join the navy together, but I backed out, and Savannah went. I was nervous about joining because I had to learn how to swim. I chose to go away to college. I chose the college that my cousin Brittany was attending. My grandparents approved of my choice, because of course, Brittany would be there to look after me.

During my college years, I began experiencing the prophetic calling upon my life. I didn't understand it at the time. I remember my best friend Jamie drove down to Macomb, Illinois to pick me up for spring break. Jamie bought her brother Edward and her cousin Kim with her. Jamie was my best friend from high school. Jamie and I got into a lot of trouble during our high school years together. We were in the car discussing all types of topics. We discussed topics that spanned from our childhoods, and early experiences, to the spiritual, and God.

During our conversation about God, I told Jamie that she should come to church with me, and that God had a message for her. She told me how nervous she was about attending church because she hadn't attended church in a very long time. I told her I would be right by her side, to hold her hand.

Now rewind back.

When I was thirteen, my mother had succumbed to her illness. After the death of my mother; my aunt Yolanda told me that God had spoken to her, and told her that I would become her daughter. Yolanda was a church goer. Yolanda is the mother of my cousin Teyanna. Yolanda became my aunt when my mothers sister Sarah, married Yolanda's brother Byron. She faithfully went to church every Sunday and every Wednesday for bible study. I joined my Auntie Yolanda along with my other cousins for church. Savannah didn't go with us. I was familiar with church. Savannah and I used to attend church with our mother at the Progressive Baptist Church on the south side of Chicago.

Progressive Baptist Church was the church my mother grew up in. We were even baptized at the age of eleven, but due to the severity of my mother's illness there were times when we would miss out on church. After my mother's death, I joined my aunt Yolanda's church. That's where I was introduced to the prophetic anointing.

I didn't understand it at first. I thought the Pastor was picking on me, so I would sit in the back of the church sometimes, to try to avoid him, and stop him from calling me out. But we all know when God has a word for you, He is going to deliver that word. No matter how many times I would sit in the back of the church, my pastor would still call me up to the altar and prophesy into my life.

Now back to the church invitation I had given to my best friend Jamie, she decided to join me. At the end of the sermon my pastor stood beside her, told her to stand up, and told me to stand up next to her, and hold her hand, which I did. He began to prophesy to her.... wow!

That's when I knew that I was hearing the voice of the Lord! Now, mind you, I was in college living my adult life. To be honest, I was not ready to answer the call God had upon my life. I still wanted to "*do me*." I felt like I was too young to answer to the call that God had on my life. I thought that christian life would be boring. So I ran for while.

CHAPTER TWO

Proceed With Caution

I was very irresponsible the first year that I went away to college. I barely went to class at all. I was away from home, with so much freedom on my hands, that I didn't care about going to class or studying. All I cared about was making sure I fit in. During my college years, I was very promiscuous, I didn't care if a guy I was interested in, had a girlfriend. All I wanted was to feel accepted at the time. I remember I went to a frat party and there was a cute guy who was a part of the fraternity. I invited him back to my room and we had sex. He didn't even ask me for my phone number and at that time, I didn't care. Due to my heavy partying, I was unable to focus on schoolwork, so I dropped out of college and went back home to Chicago.

I found a job at a bank, and I worked there for a few months. One day, on my way out of the beauty salon, I was approached by a guy. He was physically fit and drove a Mercedes Benz. His charisma was what caught my eye at that time. He was very polite, and he had a southern accent. We talked on the phone a few times.

After a few conversations, he decided to take it upon himself to ask me to take a ride with him. He didn't ask me to go out on a date but asked me to go out for a ride with him. So, I accepted his offer. We rode around for an hour, then of course we ended up at his house, and I ended up in his bed.

The next morning, he dropped me off at home. Did I hear from him again?

No.

I remember calling his phone one night and he picked up and told me never to call his phone again. I was hurt by his response, but I should've expected it, because I hadn't heard from him since that night we were together.

By the time I was 21 years old I had never experienced a relationship. Well that was about to change. I was leaving a fast food restaurant and a guy was outside waiting for me to come out. I had never seen this man before, but he was nice looking. He introduced himself as Eric. So, I gave him my name. We made small talk while standing outside the restaurant. By the end of the conversation, we exchanged numbers.

We went out to dinner at a restaurant and rode downtown, that same night. That night of course, I ended up at his apartment and of course we had sex. I spent the night with him and during the night he told me to erase every man's number I had in my phone, because he was now my man.

I was so ecstatic. The next morning, he dropped me off at home. I heard from him all that day. We texted and called each other all day long. Every night he came to my house to pick me up, so that I could spend the night with him. The first month I must say, was great. After the first month, I saw the first red flag.

I was riding in the car with my cousins and I saw Eric's car, so I sped up to speak to him, and of course he had a female in his car. He saw me, and he sped off.

Of course, me thinking with my emotions, I followed him. It was like a high-speed chase and he even crashed into my car to get away. Did I allow that first incident to end the relationship?

No!

He saw how naive I was, and manipulated his way through the entire relationship. I was so stupid, to allow myself to put up with his mess for the next three years. He was dealing with women after women. He even had a relationship, with a young lady that lived exactly two blocks away from me.

Eric had an apartment with one of his good friends, and whenever he and I would get into a fight, he would run right down to the girl's house. I knew he was down there because his car was parked in front of her house. I ignored every warning sign there was. He even proposed to me during that entire dysfunctional relationship, and I accepted it because in my head, I was number one and those chicks he was dealing with, were after me.

CHAPTER THREE

My Biggest

Blessings

After the first year of dating I was pregnant with Eric's first child. Even though I knew that he had other women, I still wanted to have his child. Those nine months of my pregnancy were hell. Eric would go missing for days without even answering his phone.

I couldn't sleep at night, and I would toss and turn all night long. When he finally appeared, he would wine and dine me with gifts to keep me satisfied. I remember the night I went into labor with our first born, Eric told me he was going to the Horse Shoe with his friends. The Horse Shoe is a casino in Hammond, Indiana.

I went into labor later that night and of course, I was unable to reach him. My best friend Draya who accompanied me to the hospital, finally got a hold of him just in the nick of time. Draya was my best friend that I met after I came home from college. We met through an old mutual friend of ours. When I met Draya she had a son named Mario, who eventually became my god son.

I was ready to push our son into the world and Eric walked right in as I was delivering. I noticed a huge hickey on his neck. I didn't address it because I wanted to focus on our new born son. To be honest, I don't believe I ever addressed it.

After our son was born, things didn't change like I thought they would. Eric was still messing with women after women, including the girl down the street. It came as no surprise that I was pregnant, for a second time. I found out I was pregnant when our oldest son was 8 weeks old.

I planned to abort this baby. I was

still living at home with my grandmother and I couldn't fathom the idea of having another baby, considering all the difficulties that Eric and I were going through. The weeks grew longer and before I knew it, I was 5 months pregnant. By that time I decided to keep my baby. My father who was out of prison now for 3 years, and my grandmother were very disappointed. I had made up in my mind that I would keep my baby. So, I did!

Eric and I finally got an apartment together, but I was barely there. I was still kind of living with my grandmother. One night I decided to stay with my grandma. I was about seven months pregnant. The next morning, I went home, and I when I went to open the door, Eric stopped me.

I had our oldest son on my hip because he was not walking at that time. I knew right then, that Eric had a woman in there. So, I forced my way through the door and saw a young lady standing there in her bra and her pants barely buttoned. I lunged at her and Eric stopped me. Of course, the young lady left.

I remember it was a Sunday

morning. I was so hurt. I decided to go on, and when our second son was born, Eric was there through the entire labor. And he didn't come in with a hickey on his neck.

After our second son was born Eric promised he would come back to stay with me in the hospital but he didn't. I called him, and he didn't answer. I felt myself going into a panic attack, and I grabbed my bible that I packed with me, and I began reading my bible. I turned on the television and Joyce Meyers was on during my stay in the hospital. I don't remember the title of her segment, but I do remember that after reading my bible, and praying, and watching Joyce Meyers, I felt a spirit of peace come over me.

After our second son was born, the physical and mental abuse grew stronger. Eric would fight me when I caught him in a lie, and we argued constantly. Once our second son was born, Eric bought another chick into our home, and things got out of hand. I knew my breaking point was near, when our second born made five months. I realized that I couldn't keep putting myself through the cheating and abuse, so I broke up with Eric. He took it hard. He would come by my house to talk to my father, and he would call my sister and my friends, but there was nothing he could do or say that would change my mind. I was fed up and done!

CHAPTER FOUR

Too Smart for My Own Good

*A*fter our break up, I decided that I needed some time to find myself, and allow myself to heal from three years of emotional stress and physical abuses. I went an entire year celibate, and finding myself, and staying connected to God. During that time, Draya had a brother that was incarcerated. Any sibling of Draya's is a sibling of mine.

Jeremiah was in jail, fighting two cases. During his time in prison, I would go and visit him along with Draya, their mother and their other siblings. Jeremiah was a hard headed little boy, growing up. He was into the street life one hundred percent. Jeremiah was 13 years old, when Draya and I became good friends. I was there to witness his stages of rebellion, and his path to self destruction.

That path led him to the prison system, fortunately. I say fortunately, because I know that God put him in prison to save his life. During the prison visits, I noticed, and honestly, I believe I was the first one to witness, the change within Jeremiah.

He didn't care about what was going on in the streets anymore. He began to care about his personal and spiritual development during his time in prison. I remember I went to visit him, and during that visit we kept staring at each other. There was a chemistry that was beginning to brew. I tried to ignore it, but later that night I decided to write to him, and tell him what I was feeling during our visit.

It was weird because he and I looked at each other as brother and sister. I was around when he had his girlfriends, and he was around when I was with my kid's father. I received his response, and to my surprise he didn't reject what I wrote him, instead he insisted that I be there for him for moral support and that we would see where this would take us.

We began to write each other more often, and I visited him more often. The chemistry grew stronger for both of us. It was something that we couldn't resist. During the time that we were building this relationship, Jeremiah was sentenced to 20 years for murder. When he took that twenty years deal, it was like the spirit of God came over me, and God revealed to me that Jeremiah will not do the entire sentence.

God revealed that this was a part of the process that God was taking him through, a process to which would lead him into his God ordained purpose. I told him that I would be there for him. But I allowed the negativity of others and their opinions to get in the way of our relationship. I had individuals telling me that he was using me, that I was selling myself short, and that I was too good for Jeremiah.

I knew deep in my heart the type of man I was dealing with, and that due to his mistakes in life, he wouldn't allow them to keep him bound.

He allowed it to make him into the man that God was calling him to be. I also believed his feelings towards me were genuine. I made a promise to be there for him, and to wait this thing out with him. But I allowed the opinions of others to cloud my vision, and I broke my promise with him. I started seeking and searching from other men the intimacy that Jeremiah couldn't fulfill.

CHAPTER FIVE

Boys in Blue

While I was searching, and seeking, I met a Chicago police officer one day while I was walking my children to school. He was in a black Tahoe coming up the wrong way on a one way street. I didn't pay any mind to it. I kept walking. Then, he stopped, and he spoke, and I spoke as well. I continued walking so his partner at the time, reversed the car, and he proceeded to hold a conversation with me.

He decided to get out the car and he introduced himself as Martin. I was perplexed at his name because on his badge it read Martin. I was wondering why he was giving me his last name and not his first name. I was enticed by his appearance though. He was psychically fit. He had on a bullet proof vest with his street clothes on, so I was enjoying looking at him.

We exchanged numbers. That day I saw Martin three times. And during those three times we couldn't keep our hands off each other. I was craving the kind of intimacy that Jeremiah couldn't give me. As our relationship grew, it pulled me away from Jeremiah. And soon enough, I stopped responding to his letters and I no longer went to visit him.

I was so in tuned with Martin. There were several red flags that appeared to me, and I addressed them with Martin, but of course he reassured me that I was overreacting. One of the red flags after a month of us seeing each other was, I didn't know where he lived. His excuse was that, he was raising his fourteen year old daughter at the time since she was one year old, and that he was not used to bringing women around her.

I accepted that excuse, and gave him the benefit of doubt. After a month of us seeing each other, he was involved in a horrible accident while on duty. He texted me at 6:30 in the morning to let me know he had been in an accident. I asked him if I could come see him. He told me that I couldn't because there were a lot of police at the hospital. I lied to my friends and told them that I went to see him, because I thought it was embarrassing to tell them that Martin had told me I couldn't visit him in the hospital. I figured they would say what I had already been suspecting, that Martin had another woman.

Jamie had a God brother who was also on the police force who went to visit his brother in blue because they were stationed in the same district. After his visit, he contacted Jamie with some interesting news. She contacted me, and filled me in on who was at the hospital, sitting next to Martin.

A young lady was introduced as his wife.

My stomach dropped, and my heart began beating so fast. I instantly got off the phone with Jamie, and I called Martin. He told me that the woman that was there, was the mother of his two boys, and that they were divorced, but she still introduced herself as his wife. I was still skeptical on his response. He even went ghost on me for a few weeks. He wouldn't answer my phone calls or text messages. I reached out to his partner Carlton and sent him a message through Facebook.

Carlton and I went to high school together. He was a few years older than me. Carlton reassured me that Martin was not married. I took his word. Mind you, I still hadn't heard from Martin. During the time that Martin was missing in action, me and Carlton started developing a friendship. We kept in contact with each other. For some odd reason our feelings started to grow for one another. I think this was happening because he was filling that void.

Remember, Martin was absent.

Carlton and I ended up at a motel together one evening and we had sex!

Wow!

I slept with this man's friend and partner. I felt so bad after it happened. I knew that was not a part of my character. I had never slept with another man's friend. Carlton was the same as Martin. I didn't know where he lived either. He was hiding something just like Martin. Carlton was taking the place of Martin. Carlton started texting and calling me every single day. He would ask me how I was feeling or how was my day going. These were the things that I needed Martin to do.

After Carlton and I's sexual encounter, Martin showed back up. I didn't tell Martin about Carlton and I. I was afraid of losing him again. To be honest I was more attracted to Martin physically and sexually. Martin and I continued our relationship, shall I say, sexual relationship. Martin was still injured, so he was not working. I saw him more, but only at my place of residence. I didn't even care to know why he abandoned me for those few months, I was just happy to have him back. I ditched Carlton. He no longer heard from me.

Out the blue one day, I got a call from Martin. He was in a rage. This was very unusual, because Martin barely called at all. We pretty much always texted. So, I knew something was wrong. He was on the phone asking me who I was sleeping with, and of course I told him 'no one'.

He proceeded to ask me again and I told him 'no one'. Then he said, "Are you sure you're not sleeping with Carlton?"

I hung up immediately. My mind started racing. How did he know? Who told him? Then the text messages started coming in. I was a slut, I lied to him, he was done with me.

Carlton had told him everything.

I was so mad at Carlton. I couldn't believe he did that to me. I was so enraged. I didn't respond to any of his messages. I went to bed that night. I was going to give him some time to cool off before I told him everything.

The next morning, I received a text message from Martin, stating that he was ready for me to tell him everything, so I did. I was still mad at Carlton because I couldn't understand why he would tell Martin about our relationship. Was Carlton mad at me and seeking revenge? I didn't contact Carlton, and I made up in my mind, I wanted to make things work with Martin.

CHAPTER SIX

My Beautiful Blessing

We continued to move forward with our relationship after Martin found out that I had had sex, with his partner. Now we were two years into our relationship, and I still didn't know where this man lived.

I was still friends with Carlton on Facebook. One day I decided to visit Carlton's page. There was a picture on one of Carlton's posts of a young lady who commented on his page, and her last name was Martin!

31

My inner woman senses became awakened, and I clicked on her page. And you can guess what I found while on her page. Her husband Mr. Matthew Martin. Matthew was his first name, remember I only called him Martin, which was his last name.

I was livid!

I was at work when I made this discovery. I had to step away from my work space, and I went straight to the bathroom. This young lady had pics of her and her husband Matthew! She had posted about him. Some were bad posts. I just couldn't look anymore.

I called him. He lied of course. Martin told me that she was a girlfriend that claimed him as her husband. I asked him if her kids were his because I saw that she had kids.

He told me no!

He said that he didn't want any kids with her. I needed a few days to ponder my thoughts. I should have known this day was going to come. I had invested two years with this man and look at me now!

Martin contacted me that night. He said he didn't care how many days I needed, he wanted to talk to me. He was working a side job at a truck stop, and he asked me if

I could come and meet him.

I did.

During that visit I cried, and I screamed and I hollered. He kept lying, then he finally told me the truth. The truth was that he was married. I was so mad at myself. I couldn't believe this was happening. He began to tell me how sorry he was, and how much he wanted to make it up to me.

We ended up having sex that night in his truck after I found out the truth, that he was a married man. I went home, and I allowed his lies to ponder in my head. Lies about his wife.

He claimed he didn't want to be with her, and that he didn't know what he was thinking, when he married her. He also said he didn't want any kids with her. His words, replayed in my head again and again. He pacified me with those statements so much and so sincerely, that I believed him.

Three months after finding out about her, I found out I was pregnant with Martin's child. He said he wanted to keep the baby, and so did I. I was afraid of what my family would think, but I soon began not care. I knew I was having his baby, and if Martin wanted this baby, then I was fine.

He was supportive during my

pregnancy. He continued to pacify me with the promise that, he was getting rid of his wife soon. I think he said that, so I wouldn't lash out at him and contact his wife, like I had threatened to do numerous times.

I began my prenatal care. My friends and family knew I was expecting. Everyone had so much to say because of his situation. I cared what they were saying but it didn't deter or discourage me. I wanted this baby and I was going to have his baby. I was enrolled in school, pursuing a degree in respiratory therapy. I was in my last semester of the program. I was determined to finish and graduate. All the odds were against me.

I was pregnant by a married man, and my family and friends were talking about it. I could've allowed it to influence me, but I didn't. I graduated at the top of my class with honors. I also received some good news as well, we were having a baby girl.

I always wanted a girl. Everyone knew it. I couldn't be happier. I wanted this to be a happy, healthy pregnancy. I didn't want to fill my mind with any nonsense. I tried not to focus on what

Martin was doing with his marriage. I wanted to focus on a healthy pregnancy. My baby girl was coming. After graduation, I began to prepare for her arrival.

Draya and my cousin Teyanna decided to throw me a baby shower. I didn't invite anyone from Martin's family. He claimed his mother and daughter knew of my pregnancy, but I didn't believe him, because all he did was lie. Our daughter was born on July 21st, 2015 and she came out so beautiful. I'm not trying to brag, but our daughter came into this world so beautiful. Martin was there of course, so he could bond with his daughter. He pretty much stayed at the hospital close to the time that visiting hours were over.

CHAPTER SEVEN

Rejection in Exchange for Protection

Our daughter was born, and our relationship continued. The birth of our daughter began to bring clarity to my situation. I began to question myself. Would I want my daughter in a relationship like this, dealing with a married man?

No!

I needed a way out. My life was not

going how I expected it to. Martin was active in our daughter's life, but his wife was still in the picture, and to me, it seemed like she wasn't going anywhere. I got one of my coworkers to send Martin a friend request to become her friend on Facebook. Because he blocked me from Facebook.

I started to snoop and spy on Martin's page. I saw a young lady on his page, commenting on his page like *'hey bae'*, *'I love you'*. And it wasn't his wife.

Curious, and suspicious, I went on her page, and she was talking about her man, Martin. I couldn't believe it! I thought to myself, are you kidding me? She even had a picture of Martin sitting on her couch.

This young lady appeared to be young, very young. She looked as though she was almost the age of his daughter, who was eighteen years old by now. She was posting on her page, praising Martin and saying how much he meant to her, and how much he does for her and her children.

I was so livid.

I called Martin immediately, and of course, he had an excuse for everything. He claimed that this young lady was just his friend.

LOL.

I was not stupid. He finally told me all about her, after weeks of me questioning him about her. He finally decided to tell me that he was seeing her, over a text message. He didn't tell me face to face. I cursed him, I called him every curse word. I was angry, but really, deep down, I already knew. I was not about to come second to this little girl, as well as his wife.

I had enough.

I told him, I was done. It hurt me so bad.

Martin began to become verbally abusive towards me, after I found out about her. He started telling me that I was mad that he didn't choose me, and that I knew what the relationship was, when I had gotten pregnant. He said that I was mad and angry and bitter.

So, I lashed out on him in return. I threatened to not allow him to see his child, and told him that he would never see his daughter again. I said those things because I was being spiteful, and angry. I got so angry, that I decided to take matters into my own hands, and decided to contact his wife.

I had had enough. Our daughter was still a secret, and I didn't care. Our daughter didn't deserve to be a secret any longer.

I contacted Martin's wife via Facebook.

She had no clue of our daughter's existence. She said that she knew about the little girl that Martin was dealing with.

Martin had pushed me to my limit. I let her know all about our daughter. Before I revealed everything, our daughter had never been to her father's house. After the contact with Martin's wife, our daughter was over their house a lot more.

Martin's wife began to stress about how she was tired of him and his horrible ways. She ended the conversation via Facebook messenger by saying that my daughter had another sibling on the way. I asked Martin about it, and he said that she was supposedly pregnant with his baby, but that he didn't know if the baby was actually his. I thought to myself, "Are you serious?"

The lies that this man was telling, were hilarious. I began to wonder what lies he was telling about our daughter.

I needed to find an outlet, so I resorted to being sexually involved with other women. In the beginning of our relationship, Martin told me how much it turned him on for two women to be together sexually. At first, I declined, but he kept insisting. He wanted a threesome, so one day I gave him one.

To be honest, I enjoyed it. That

experience actually opened the door to me being involved with other women. I just wanted Martin to accept me. I wanted him to see that I was a "down" chick for him, but I was tearing myself down.

I had lost focus on my values, and my beliefs. After I found out about the other women he was involved with, I needed an outlet, so I looked for it in sexual contact with women. I think I also did it to make him mad, because I knew that if he knew I was messing with other women, and he couldn't be involved in it, he would get mad. I was breaking myself down more and more. I was not focused on my kids or my career. I needed a change.

God was talking but I was not listening.

One Friday night, Draya and I decided to attend my cousin's church. My cousin Keisha was a church pastor, and it was prophetic night Friday. She talked about how rejection is for our protection. I felt like that message was for me. The rejection that I was getting from my daughter's father, was for my protection. The door that I was trying to keep open, God was closing, and closing it for a reason, and that reason was in my best interest.

I cried the entire time she was preaching. She closed the night by prophesying to Draya. She told Draya that it was time for her to relocate to a different city, and to start her new business venture.

That was my moment.

That night we made up our minds, that we were moving to Atlanta. We had already talked about it, but we just didn't know when. Once God confirmed it, we knew that was our cue. I knew that moving would be a great way to remove myself from my situation.

I had to leave. Draya started looking for houses. She found one. My family didn't believe that I was leaving, but I knew it was the best thing for both myself, and my children. Chicago was so violent. Every day, Chicago made national news on the violence that plagued our city. The school year was nearing an end, so I decided to wait until the kid's school year was over, before relocating.

My family took it hard, especially my grandmother. I was very close to my grandmother. My children were close to her as well. It really affected her when she found out that I was moving. She would ask me if I sure was about this. She thought I was making the wrong decision. She also expressed how much she would miss my kids.

The school year ended, and I still hadn't found a job in my profession in Atlanta, but I didn't care. The lease was up at the house I was staying. I put my two weeks' notice in at my job, and on June 26th my children and I boarded our flight to Atlanta. I knew that once my children and I were walking on that plan, my life was in God's hands. No longer was I in control of it.

God was finally in control.

CHAPTER EIGHT

New Beginnings

We made it! Atlanta. Draya, and her kids, myself and my kids, in total we had six kids.

We didn't have a plan, well, we thought we had a plan, but God had a bigger plan for us.

My cousin Tasha, who is also a minister, had reached out to me, because she knew that I would be relocating to Georgia. She had a cousin, Pastor Karen Jones, who had her own church in Georgia. I was a little hesitant because I wasn't eager to suddenly join a church so soon, or so I thought.

It was my first week in Georgia, and

Tasha contacted me and told me to reach out to her other cousin Tanya, who would put me in contact with the pastor she had been telling me about.I contacted Tanya, and we were on the phone for a long time. We talked about our callings and how the much-anointed pastor Karen, and her husband Apostle Larry Jones were. We talked about how Pastor Karen, she went by the name PK would push you to your God ordained purpose and destiny.

I knew then, that we needed to visit that church soon. I told Draya all about it, and she was excited as well. We went to their church anniversary service. When we walked into the sanctuary, we could feel the anointing all over the room.

On this Sunday they had a guest speaker, and he *preached* that sermon. After he preached the sermon he called for prayer, so of course, me and Draya went to the alter and PK and Apostle laid hands on us.

They began to pray for us, and prophesy to us. It was like a tag team. After the prayer they asked if anyone wanted to join, and me and Dray couldn't resist, we joined.

Understand, that I have never joined a church on my first visit, but this was a totally different experience for me and for Draya, as well. We attended church faithfully. Pastor Karen was not only a pastor, but she was also a life coach, and mentor. I was still in between jobs. I was waiting for the state of Georgia to approve my license, so that I could work in my profession.

My money was running low. PK also had a broadcast that she would do weekly on a social website called Periscope. Her broadcast was called the daily declarations(DDZ). We would declare the word of God, and apply it to our lives.

Every morning Draya and I would tune in. PK was feeding our spirits daily. After the broadcast was over, we would be fueled up, and ready to tackle our tasks and goals for the day. PK had announced that she would be offering a mentoring program. She would mentor a certain number of women for thirteen weeks, and during the thirteen weeks she would help us accomplish our goals.

We knew we had to join. I didn't care what the cost would be, I just knew this was something I needed. We eagerly joined the group. I would sew my last into this class, but I knew it was for a good cause. During my season of unemployment, I had to make myself useful. An idle mind is the devil's workshop. So, one day on the DDZ,

PK began to prophesy. She said that it was time for women to hear my story. It was time for my ministry to come forth, and women needed to hear how I overcame my afflictions. Draya and I looked at each other, and I knew it was time for me to get out there and tell my story.

I started doing a live broadcast on Facebook live. The first live I did attracted at least 1500 views. I was nervous during my first broadcast. But I got my message out there, and people started inboxing me, and telling me how inspired they were by my story.

I was so encouraged, so I continued to do the Facebook live sessions. A high school friend of mine had a women's ministry, doing prayer conference calls weekly, and she would have a special speaker each week. She asked me if I could be her speaker for the week. I accepted the request.

During the prayer call I heard the lord say it's time for me to be transparent, so I told my story on how I had a baby by a married man, and how I was involved in bisexual relationships with other women. After I shared my story with the other women on the call, the line was opened for comments and questions.

I'll tell you, those women of God poured into my life. They were prophesying to me. One of the women said she could see me with an all women ministry and that she sees me speaking to so many women, sharing my story, and telling my testimony.

She also said it was time for my ministry to come forth, and that the blood of young women was on my hands. Another woman prophesied to me and told me to start preparing myself for my husband, and start letting God know what it is I want in my husband, including how I want him to be with my children, and what type of character I want him to possess.

After that call I was in tears and over joyed. I knew it was time to fulfill all that God had in store for me. During the finish, in this strong mentoring group, PK had us write down three goals we wanted to fulfill before the new year. Mine were to find a job, launch my all women ministry, and start working on my book.

We met weekly to discuss how we were moving towards our goals, and we would also discuss different topics like spirituality, personal development, and relationships. A week into the session, I began getting phone calls requesting interviews. God was surely moving, and He was moving fast.

I had finally gotten my license, and it took months for anyone to contact me for an interview, but the interviews started coming. It was time for me to choose a name for the all women ministry as well. I also had to come up with a marketing strategy.

Draya helped me come up with the name H.E.A.L for the ministry. Heal means, Healing, Empowering one another, Accepting, accepting the past, and changing Lives all under the leadership of God.

PK insisted that I needed to start a Facebook group, so I started the group, and in two weeks over five hundred women joined the group. I received so many messages on how much this group was needed, and how it was helping so many women.

I would post a "share your story" every Thursday, and women would share their stories. I even decided to start different chapters, in Chicago, Atlanta, and Florida.

I met two young ladies by the name of Danielle and Keona. Danielle lived in Chicago, and Keona lived in Florida. These young ladies were some prayer warriors. I had to connect with them.

HEAL Ministry had monthly prayer calls and bible study. We even had our first Panel Discussion, *"From Trials to Triumph Victorious Women."*

Those panel discussions turned into prophetic panel discussions. I had my brother in Christ, that I met through a mutual friend of ours who went by the name Dee, say a prayer for the women from the men. It was an amazing experience. Keona had invited her god parents from Florida to join us. The man of God and his wife, literally allowed the holy spirit to use them.

Lives were changed, women were healed, and delivered. DEE invited some people to join him. I didn't know that one of the individuals he brought, would form a true connection with me, but I'll save that for the next chapter. I returned to Atlanta on fire. I had no idea that within a few months, things would transpire and I would make a drastic decision.

CHAPTER NINE

Trusting God in the Midst of It All

Life started getting pretty hard for us back in Atlanta. Draya decided to move back home, once her kids were done with school. But I decided to stick it out. I had gotten myself and the kids an apartment closer to the city of Atlanta. My cousin who had previously moved to Atlanta, decided to move in with me, which would help me financially with the rent. A friend of mine lived in Marietta Georgia, and she was willing to help me with my kids.

I put my kids in school with her son, while she kept my daughter. Financially and physically, it became a drain. I would drive every morning before work to drop my kids off at her house, then head to work. This was a thirty minute drive daily. I began to get overwhelmed. Her mother even decided to move down to Atlanta to help. Still the heavy burden I was carrying, was not lifted. Too many times, I've put others before myself and I always got the short end of the stick.

It was a new year and I decided I would no longer put others happiness first. It was time to put my happiness first, so decided to move back home to Chicago where my strong support system resided.

My family was so excited. My children's fathers were excited as well. I struggled with this decision because in a sense, I didn't want to seem like a failure, returning home.

I had a talk with my big cousin Torrance, who reassured me that I had to make the best choice for my children, and not to beat myself up about it. That conversation surely did help. My grandmother was happy as well. She really took it hard when we moved to Atlanta, so when she found out we were moving back, I knew she would welcome us with open arms.

I sent my children first, then I would surely follow. I had contacted my old boss, to let her know I was returning back home and I needed my job back. Of course, she rehired me. I found an apartment on the east side of Chicago and I was back home.

Now, being back home was a bit of a struggle, I must admit, because of the familiar spirits that started coming back around. I started to think, Lord am I ready? Maybe I should have stayed back in Atlanta. The spirit of loneliness started creeping and I started talking again to a few people I had severed ties with.

I started making plans to meet up with these individuals. On Valentine's day I was at a vegan restaurant ordering some food, and I ran into a young man that I had met at my women's panel discussion, a young man that I met through DEE. We spoke and made eye contact, but I didn't think he knew exactly who I was.

His name was Wade. We were

friends on social media, so I decided to hit him up, just to let him know that I saw him in the restaurant, and I admired what he was doing, and that I was keeping him covered in prayer. Wade was an activist in the community, very well-known, and he had some ventures he was getting ready to start. Oddly, we exchanged numbers and starting conversing.

Some days I would text to see how he was doing, and he would do likewise. Then one day I invited him over to my house. Now, normally I don't do this because my children were home, but he was a bit of an exception, because I didn't really look at Wade like that, and I didn't think he looked at me like that either.

Now, don't get me wrong, Wade was fine, but I never looked at him as someone I could potentially date, not even when I first met him at my event. Anyway, we sat on my couch and we talked for hours until the late hours. Of course, the flesh started kicking in and I asked him if he wanted to have sex.

He told me that he was waiting for marriage.

WOW.

I had been on this celibate journey, and I finally found someone who was celibate like me. All this time I thought I had to settle, that there were no men out there that were celibate like me. So, we fell asleep on my couch and we woke before the kids woke and he left.

Now I don't think Wade is the man God has for me. I truly believe God was showing me my hearts desires and reminding me that I don't have to settle at all. God has his best, just for me. So as I continue this purity journey until marriage, I know God is still writing my love story.

I know God has someone out there who will love me, the woman I am, and my children. I don't have to settle and dummy down, to feel accepted by a man. I know that everything will work out well for me, and for my good, because I love God, and I was called according to His purpose.

Everything I went through was for a purpose, and when I'm standing in front of my King, I will know why it never worked out with the rest, because God was saving me for his best. Even my own testimony is the door for another woman's breakthrough.

I want you to know that life is going to present trials and tribulations, but it's how you allow God to use you in those trials, all for His glory. I been in some messes, but I know it was no one, but the hand of God who kept me in the midst of it all.

I'm home now, around my family, who really love me and my children. My grandmother, has been my biggest supporter, and thankfully, God has truly been keeping her, to help me with my children. I have my support system back, and my children have their fathers, and their other siblings back in their lives. My father has been clean now for five years.

To God be the glory!!!!!

I don't understand what God is doing this season, but whatever it is, I surrender to His will, and His way. Stay tuned for part two, you never know, it may be my book on how I met my husband.

Thank you for allowing me to share my story with you.

I love each and every one of you.

ABOUT GENINA JOHNSON

Genina Johnson is a single mother of 3, Alex, Excell Jr. and Mckenzie , born and raised in Chicago, IL.
She is a respiratory therapist who is now obtaining her bachelor's degree in Business Leadership from Ashford University.

She is the founder and CEO of the Non-profit organization, H.E.A.L Ministry. Genina is also a member of All Nations Worship Assembly, Chicago. She is not only a physical lifesaver, but she is a spiritual lifesaver, helping God's daughters be healed and set free from things that have held them bound.

A Note From Genina

My testimony displays the redemption of God and the strong God fearing woman that He made to conquer every trial and tribulation that was bought my way. This book Purpose in my Pain entails the things that I went through as a young child into my adult life. Things that should've taken me out but drew my closer to Him. Things that will give other women hope that you too will make it!

That you too have a story and that you too was born with God ordain purpose. Don't be shamed of your past because your past prepares you for the future that God has in store for you.

Keep going my sister your testimony is the the key to another woman's breakthrough!

www.geninaj.com

www.ingramcontent.com/pod-product-compliance
Lightning Source LLC
Chambersburg PA
CBHW060557100426
42742CB00013B/2590